T0365363

ARMISTICE DAY

100 YEARS

NGAIRE PERCIVAL

Print information available on the last page

Rev. date: 12/21/2018

To order additional copies of this book, contact:
Xlibris
0800-443-678
www.xlibris.co.nz
Orders@ Xlibris.co.nz

ARMISTICE DAY

100 YEARS

ANZAC COVE GALLIPOLI 1915.

"WE WILL REMEMBER THEM"

THE LEAVING.
They hated leaving their mates behind.
They hated leaving them alone.
They had no choice they had to go.
They felt as though they deserted their dead friend.
It broke many hearts, time was at end.

THE FIRST WORLD WAR.

THE LANDING TO THE LEAVING FROM GALLIPOLI.

On the 25th of April 1915 the Australian and New Zealand Army Corp united as the ANZAC.

From the 25th of April 1915 right up until the 19th of December 1915, after 8 horrific months ANZAC evacuated safely over 9 nights and days from Gallipoli to Egypt and Western Front, where ½ of the ANZAC'S, died.

THE LANDING.

Where a mistake to put soldiers' lives at stake.
The soldiers were shot in the barges, shot in the sea.
Shot everywhere, no matter where they be.
They were shot for liberty.

GALLIPOLI Date. 25th April 1915.

Australian and New Zealand troops land at Gallipoli....
Time. 4:35am first boat 40 men, 3 made it...
200 Turks on beach waiting for allies...
65'000 Turks on beach ridge...
What a massacre.

The BOYS –the TORTURE –the TORMENT of HELL...
What a story these young boys must tell.

SACRIFICE SENTENCED TO DIE ANZAC'S.

The New Zealand Expeditionary Forces were sent from Egypt to the Dardanelles, Turkey, to siege the capital city Constantinople, known as Istanbul today.

AUSTRALIA and NEW ZEALAND were only a meagre group, so we will send the Australians and New Zealanders over to capture the capital of Turkey.
The British Empire choose New Zealanders and the Australians as we were just an insignificant group.

Australia lost 8709 and New Zealand 2701. 11,410 ANZACS died at GALLIPOLI.

THE ANZACS WERE ORDERED TO DIE, TO DEFEND OUR COUNTRY AT ALL COST. AT ALL COSTS YOU MUST DEFEND THIS GROUND. DO NOT RETREAT. YOU MUST KEEP GOING FORWARD. YOU WILL BE USED AS AN EXAMPLE IF YOU RUN. YOU WILL BE SHOT AT DAWN. BEFORE THE RISING SUN...

I WANT YOU!

Lord Kitchener and First Admiral Mr Winston Churchill decided to go it alone, without approval as Parliament was up in arms.

GET OVER TOP

BUT IT'S NOT OUR FIGHT WE SHOULD STOP.
They were shot.

ON AN ADVENTURE. A call of duty, corpses, comrades, decomposed mates, dead, bloated, blackened, scorched all fallen to fate, over the top mate, fix bayonets, 1,2,3, whistle blow, CHARGE, oh my GOD to late.

The soldiers they stood all over DEATH.
They had no choice they were forced to stand on their comrade's head.
The Troupes they became a walking corpse, a walking dead.
My GOD how I wonder what went through those young boy's heads.

I CAN FEEL THEIR ANGUISH, I CAN FEEL THEIR DREAD.
I CAN FEEL ALL COMPOSITION GOING THROUGH A SOLDIER'S HEAD.
I AM IN TOTAL EMPATHY, I AM IN TOTAL AWE.
ALL BECAUSE OF WHAT I KNOW NOW, IS NOT WHAT I KNEW BEFORE.
ABOUT THE SHORT-COMINGS OF THE FIRST WORLD WAR.

I PRAY TO GOD to Bless the Souls of the nine and a half million people, involved in THE Great War and the 500 nurses from ANZAC.

They would have wandered, helplessly, shell shocked disorientated amongst this spread; of blue, blown up, black, rotting, dry reaching from the stench of death.

The aromatic stench of decomposing human flesh would become part of the soldier's daily psyche.

Decay in all things gross in nature's way.

Oh my GOD those poor souls.

Know nothing of progress, nothing of their upcoming death.

IT WOULD HAVE BEEN ABSOLUTLY HORRIFICE FOR THEM ALL.

GOD REST THEIR SOULS
I AM APPALLED.

It makes my blood curl.
The thoughts of their blood swirl.
Body parts in a hurl.
Do not worry, everything will be all right.
What am I doing here? Why did I enlist?

I had to defend my country, I had to show my fist.
I didn't resist.
And now my Mon cries for me.
Please tell her not to worry I'm as happy as can be.

Help me my foot is gone, it rotted from the wet socks I had on.
I'm in great pain, I feel insane, sorry mate no spare morphine.

My guts are burning, I've got dysentery, I've got many ailments hanging
around me, GOD please don't let me fall in the latrine.

The FLIES the MAGGOTS the RATS the LICE.
All things negative, not nice.

The trance of warfare.
A tennis court size of wicked demise.
5-600 men going neck for neck.
They used their bayonets.
They used their hands.
They bludgeoned each other.

They were physically enter-twined.
They were choking each other.
They were completely out of mind.
The tough survived through slaughtering each other.
The soldiers from both sides, many injured, to many died.

SACRIFICE + EMPATHY.

Post-Traumatic Stress Disorder, Obsessive Compulsive Disorder.
Intrusive horrific thoughts forever flickering.
Sacrifice and Empathy: to know what Post Traumatic Stress Disorder
can do.
I have been diagnosed with PTSD too.
P.T.S.D. O.C.D well that is me.
I am walking talking book of PTSD and OCD.

                                    Now given the chance to show my grief.
To the ever-lasting ANZAC who died in belief.
Thousands of young men, boy's father's son, grand –fathers, grand-sons.
All signed up and then died in relief.
What were they thinking.
Who died blinking as their bodies were blown away.
Some are thinking my GOD what is happening here.

God rest their Souls that vaporized in the air.

"WE WILL REMEMBER THEM"

SACRIFICE + EMPATHY.

SENTENCED TO DIE.

SENTENCED TO DEATH.

ALL IN THE MAKING OF HISTORY.

END OF STORY.

THERE IS NOTHING MORE TO SAY.

SACRIFICE + EMPATHY

My mini war field of Gallipoli being a blackboard that became the base of my construction and in the middle a sandbox reveals World War 1 in miniature 3D.

1. The cover of the magazine The Illustrated War News, 1915 is an introduction in my world of grief, despair, disbelief of what happened from 1914-1918?

THE FIRST WORLD WAR - GALLIPOLI.

2. The periscope in the old railway track pin holder brings you closer to what is laid down in front of you.
3. The sea has many black war ships and 3 Red Cross Hospital Ships needed to care for the wounded.
4. WE WANT YOU!
5. The TOP represents going's "OVER THE TOP". It was a 6 second window go now or else you got shot.
6. The LANDING BAY became a disastrous encounter with DEATH.
7. DEATH GREETED THE SOLDIERS.
8. THE TURKS WERE FULLY PREPARED WITH 200 ON THE BEACH SHORE AND 65,000 WAITING ON THE RIDGES FOR THE GLORY OF WAR.
9. The CHESS pieces show the STALEMATE of the Bloody War.
10. The magnetic white board has become a back board for displaying 3 stages of WORLD WAR 1, the bottom picture is the sea.

Bottom picture shows the ships at sea waiting to bomb Gallipoli.

The Middle section is the Landing at Gallipoli, SLAUGHTER IN THE SEA.

And the top image show Soldiers waiting for action, a dead Turk in a Trench and a BOMB exploding near a ship docked on a small pier.

11. The Mirror reflects the HELL OFF WAR.

Execution of 306 British troops were shot for being cowards, 5 of them were ANZACS. They call it "Setting an example" a deterrent from running away.

12. SLAUGHTER of the ANZAC.
13. The LEAVING OF GALLIPOLI. In the TRENCH they go, silence is of importance, we must not let Jonny Turk know that we are going to go with-out telling them.

NOT ONE SOLDIER DIED IN LEAVING GALLIPOLI.

The ANZACS WENT TO EGYPT WHERE HALF OF THEM FELL.

14. The PYRAMID indicates their ongoing saga of their continuous hell.
15. The WHISTLE, the dreaded whistle, one two three blow, here we go, OVER THE TOP, OH MY GOD WHAT A GRIMLY SHOW.
16. WE WILL REMEMBER THEM trophy
17. The (2) Brodie Helmets are from World War 2.
18. The VICTORIAN TOWEL RACK converted into a WOODEN CROSS. The CONNECTION is SPIRITUAL between ALL OBJECTS in the complete STRUCTURE of this ANZAC construction. Peace be with you.
19. The SOLDIERS BIBLE has printed on it ON ACTIVE SERVICE NZ 1918. The soldier who owned this Bible who went to War has left a BLOOD SPOT on the CORNER of his BIBLE I knew this soldier and in respect to his family, I HAVE SEALED HIS BIBLE, it is obvious on the first page because of rubbing out of this soldier's name in this Bible it is TO REMAIN SEALED. Rest in Peace.
20. The ANZAC biscuit was part of the soldier's diet.
21. The 100th year commemorative Book of ST John in remembrance of WW1.
22. An Airforce badge from the Royal New Zealand Air Force.
23. The Iron Sacrifice Cross in remembrance of WW1.
24. The New Zealand RSA commemorative badge 100 years.
25. (2) Poppies and a commemorative LEST WE FORGET badge.

26. The (4) coloured RIBBONS on the Wodden Cross.

The (1st) first ribbon is for Bravery.
The (2nd) ribbon is the 1914 Star / the Mons Star.
Four New Zealanders received this award. Two were nurse and two were New Zealand Officers.
Colonel Richard Hutton Davies and Major George Spafford Richardson – both officers were promoted to the rank of Major-General.
The (3rd) ribbon is The Brittish War Medal 1914-1920.
The (4th) ribbon is The Victory Medal 1914-1918.

27. A very old Returned Services Man badge.

THE SANDBOX.

ARMISTIST DAY.

On the 11th day of 11th month at exactly 11 am the world stood still.
THE FIRST WORLD WAR ENDED.

After 4 long years an armistice was finally agreed upon.
The war ended with Big Ben tolling over London.
The city exploding with cheer. Laughter, beer.
Music, song, dancing, tears, realization of the now.
Peace was finally here.

The encouragement to develop my talents with passion is over whelming and soul searching. This has been the best therapy yet to help me overcome my own Post Traumatic Stress Disorder, as the realities of THE FIRST WORLD WAR are unforgettable, unforgivable, unbelievable, and certainly an eyeopener, GOD REST THEIR SOULS. AMEN.

Printed in the United States
By Bookmasters